Changing Shores

By Pamela Jennett

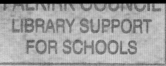

Contents

Where Land Meets Water   3

How Shores Change   6

A Changing Shoreline in Yorkshire   12

The Power of Storms   18

For Ever Changing   22

Glossary   23

Index   24

Where Land Meets Water

From space the Earth looks like a blue planet. It looks blue because its surface is mainly covered by water. All the land on Earth is surrounded by the water.

All pieces of land have **shores** where the land meets the ocean or sea. This is called the shoreline or coastline.

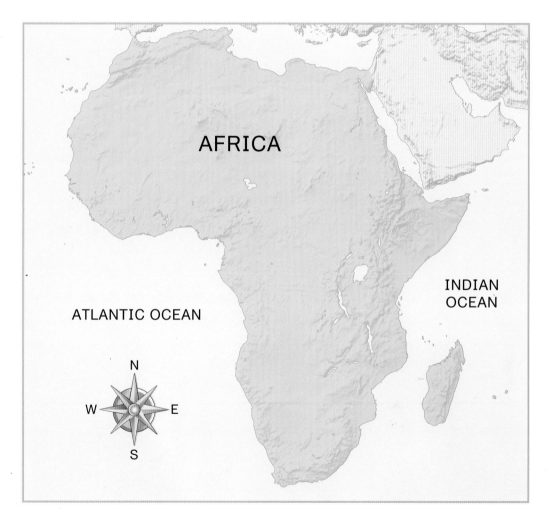

Africa is surrounded by a shoreline.

Most pieces of land are made up of many countries. Some countries have a shoreline and others do not.

Bolivia and Paraguay do not have a shoreline.

How Shores Change

Shores change all the time. The wind and the ocean waves pound against the land. They wear away the rock. This action is called **erosion**.

These rocks will erode over time.

Sometimes erosion makes a sandy beach.
This happens when waves pick up rocks, pebbles
and grit from the shore. Waves grind them
together so they break apart into small pieces.
These small pieces of rock make up sand.

A sandy shoreline changes shape all the time.
Sand is shifted by the wind and ocean waves.
This forms a different shaped shoreline.

The patterns on this beach show how
the sand has shifted.

sand spit

Sometimes as the sand shifts, it builds up along the shoreline. This forms a long, thin **sand spit**. If the wind blows sand high up on the shore, then it forms a **sand dune**.

a sand dune

9

Some shorelines are made up of rocks and cliffs. Water and wind wear away the softer rock. This leaves the harder rock behind.

arch

stack

Sometimes rough waves cut into rock and form caves and **arches**. After a long time some arches collapse. This leaves a **stack** behind.

A Changing Shoreline in Yorkshire

Most changes to the shorelines take hundreds or thousands of years. However, sometimes a shoreline changes overnight.

N

Great Britain

Holderness Coast

In Yorkshire the Holderness Coast changes all the time. Every year about two metres of shoreline erodes into the sea. During the last 2,000 years the shore has **receded** by almost 400 metres.

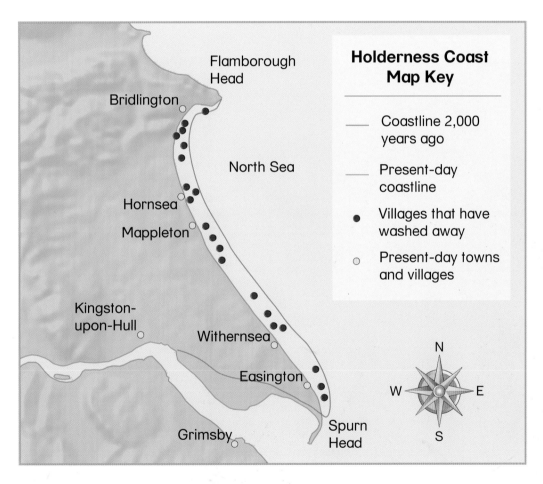

Many villages along the Holderness Coast have been washed into the sea.

Along the Holderness Coast the cliffs are very soft. The rock cracks easily and breaks away. The cliffs then slide into the water and get washed away by rough storm waves.

People live and work on the cliffs above the shore. When the cliffs break away, streets, homes and buildings fall into the North Sea.

At one time Owthorne Church stood at the edge of the crumbling cliffs. But the shoreline kept receding. Now the church is under the North Sea.

The Holderness Coast changes every day. People who live near the coast try to protect their homes from the constant erosion.

People build walls to help protect the shoreline and their homes.

The Power of Storms

Sometimes **hurricanes** change shores quickly. They are also called **cyclones**. These storms start over warm, tropical oceans. When a hurricane moves over the shore and onto the land, it is very dangerous.

In 1992 Hurricane Andrew hit the United States. The storm moved across Florida and along the Gulf Coast. It was one of the worst hurricanes to ever strike that area.

Hurricane Andrew

This satellite photograph shows the size of Hurricane Andrew.

On 26th August 1992 Hurricane Andrew pounded many islands off the coast of Louisiana. Wind, rain and waves changed the shores of many of them.

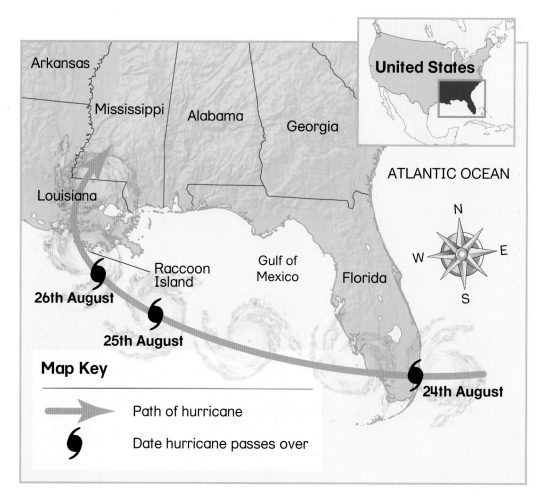

Hurricane Andrew moved from the Atlantic Ocean to the Gulf of Mexico.

One of the islands affected was Raccoon Island. Its beach was washed away during the hurricane and the shoreline changed almost overnight.

Before Hurricane Andrew

After Hurricane Andrew

For Ever Changing

The Earth's shorelines are always changing. Usually the changes are slow. Sometimes the changes are quick. These changes make each shore different.

Glossary

arches curved structures that go across an open space

cyclones tropical storms with very strong winds and heavy rain

hurricanes large storms with strong winds and heavy rain

erosion to wear away by water or wind

receded moved back or away from

sand dune a mound or ridge of sand built up on the shore

sand spit a narrow point of land that extends into the water

shores land along the edge of the sea

stack part of rock left behind after an arch collapses

Index

arches 11, 23
Atlantic Ocean 4, 5
beach 8, 21
cliffs 10, 14–16
cyclones 18, 23
erosion 6, 7, 17, 23
Holderness Coast 12–17
hurricane 18–21, 23
Hurricane Andrew 19–21
Indian Ocean 4
North Sea 13, 15, 16
Owthorne Church 16
Pacific Ocean 5
Raccoon Island 20, 21
stack 11, 23
sand 7, 8, 9
sand dune 9, 23
sand spit 9, 23
waves 6, 7, 11, 14, 20